how to be human

CLARITY PUBLISHERS
BIRMINGHAM, AL

Copyright © 2009 + Clarity Publishers

No part of this publication may be reproduced in any form without the prior written permission of the publisher except in the case of brief quotations within critical articles and reviews.

Unless otherwise noted, all Scripture quotations are taken from the Holy Bible, New International Version. Copyright © 1973, 1978, 1984 by International Bible Society. Used by permission. All rights reserved.

Printed in the United States of America.

Life Bible Study
P. O. Box 36040
Birmingham, AL 35236

To order additional copies of this resource, call the publisher at 877.265.1605 or order online at www.lifebiblestudy.com.

ROBERTA WATSON

Roberta Watson is a graduate of New Orleans Baptist Theological Seminary (NOBTS) and has served as an adjunct professor at the NOBTS North Georgia extension center. With nearly 20 years of ministry experience, she has served in a variety of educational ministries in churches in Texas and Georgia. She has also partnered with State and local Baptist Associations to provide leadership support and training to the local church.

Roberta has worked as a free-lance writer for many years providing curriculum materials for several national organizations. She has also worked as an editor of Bible curriculum and has written extensively for Clarity Publishers.

She and her husband, Todd, have been married for more than 20 years. Their daughter, Katie, is a college student, and their son, Will, is a high school student. They enjoy supporting their kids' school, extracurricular, and church activities. Her favorite vacation experience was watching the sunrise over the Sea of Galilee.

EDITORAL & DESIGN STAFF

EDITOR
Margie Williamson

COPY EDITOR
Jason Odom

ART DIRECTOR
Brandi Etheredge

GRAPHIC DESIGNER
Laurel-Dawn Berryhill

Table of CONTENTS

WEEK ONE
DEVELOPING character

WEEK TWO
THE PERFECT RESPONSE to hatred

WEEK THREE
SERVING WITH pure motives

WEEK FOUR
KINGDOM FOCUSED AND worry free

WEEK FIVE
THE DANGERS OF judging others

WEEK SIX
BUILDING FAITH foundations

how to use this book

This study has been designed to help you prepare for a group Bible Study experience, to use during a group Bible Study experience, or as an individual Bible study guide. Every lesson is divided into five sections; each section concludes with a devotional suggestion and journaling activity. To get the most from this study, consider the following suggestions:

1. Gather your favorite Bible, a pen or pencil, and a highlighter before you begin. As you study the lesson, stop and read the assigned passage first. You will have the opportunity to dig deeper into some verses at the end of each section.

2. Use the learner commentary and sidebars to guide your personal Bible study.

3. Complete each day's study with the devotional suggestions and journaling assignments at the end of each section. Allow God this time to transform you through your study and your time with Him.

4. Take your book along to your small group study. The discussion suggestions will be helpful to you during your study time.

Be prepared to consider, examine, and evaluate God's Word as you move through this study. Our prayer is that this study will give you the opportunity to better understand what God had in mind when He designed us to be human.

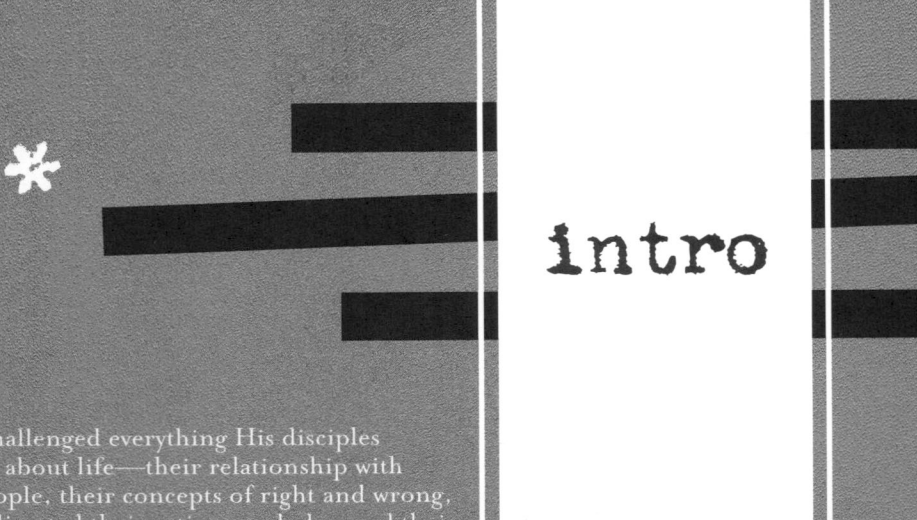

intro

Jesus frequently challenged everything His disciples thought they knew about life—their relationship with God and other people, their concepts of right and wrong, the attitudes that directed their actions each day, and their understanding of God's requirements for righteous living. Rather than maintaining the status quo, Jesus turned their world upside down, revealing that Kingdom living required a higher level of commitment from His disciples.

Jesus challenged His disciples to develop the character traits that would distinguish them as followers of God. Instead of falling into acceptable patterns of human behavior, Jesus' followers were called to be meek, merciful, holy, and set apart for God's purposes. When their lives reflected God's character, they would become walking testimonies of God's glory and point others to Him.

Because Jesus knew that those who followed Him would face hatred and persecution, He emphasized the importance of responding with love to their enemies. When followers of Christ give up their rights to vengeance, they have the opportunity to reveal His love to a world filled with hurt and hatred.

The religious leaders of the first century publicly displayed their devotion to God by calling attention to their acts of worship. Jesus emphasized that true worship begins in the hearts of His followers and is best expressed in personal and private moments spent in God's presence.

Jesus urged His followers to develop a single-minded devotion to Him and to His kingdom. He warned them of the dangers of pursuing material wealth and the futility of worrying about their future needs. Jesus promised to provide everything they need in this life and in the life to come.

For those disciples who passionately embraced His calling, Jesus cautioned His followers to remove all sinful behaviors from their own lives before pointing out the sins of others. His words reminded His followers that all people have sinned and need God's forgiveness.

Finally, Jesus assured His disciples that putting the things they learned from Him into practice would enable them to build their faith to withstand the storms of life. People were not meant to stand alone, but were designed to rely upon God in all circumstances.

Everyone who heard Jesus recognized that He spoke with great authority. Even though His teachings were radically different than previous messages delivered by the religious leaders of the day, those who became His followers realized that His words brought life to the human spirit. By following His teachings, His disciples discovered how to be human—fully human according to God's design for His creation.

8 ESSENTIAL TRUTHS

GOD IS
Only one true and living God exists. He is the Creator of the universe, eternally existing in three Persons—the Father, Son, and Holy Spirit—each equally deserving of humanity's worship and obedience. He is infinite and perfect in all His attributes.

THE BIBLE IS GOD'S WORD
The Bible is God's written revelation to people, divinely given through human authors who were inspired by the Holy Spirit. It is entirely true. The Bible is totally sufficient and completely authoritative for matters of life and faith. The goal of God's Word is the restoration of humanity into His image.

PEOPLE ARE GOD'S TREASURE
God created people in His image for His glory. They are the crowning work of His creation. Yet every person has willfully disobeyed God—an act known as sin—thus inheriting both physical and spiritual death and the need for salvation. All human beings are born with a sin-nature and into an environment inclined toward sin. Only by the grace of God through Jesus Christ can they experience salvation.

JESUS IS GOD AND SAVIOR
Jesus is both fully God and fully human. He is Christ, the Son of God. Born of a virgin, He lived a sinless life and performed many miracles. He died on the cross to provide people forgiveness of sin and eternal salvation. Jesus rose from the dead, ascended to the right hand of the Father, and will return in power and glory.

THE HOLY SPIRIT IS GOD & EMPOWERER
The Holy Spirit is supernatural and sovereign, baptizing all believers into the Body of Christ. He lives within all Christians beginning at the moment of salvation and then empowers them for bold witness and effective service as they yield to Him. The Holy Spirit convicts individuals of sin, uses God's Word to mature believers into Christ-likeness, and secures them until Christ returns.

SALVATION IS BY FAITH ALONE
All human beings are born with a sin nature, separated from God, and in need of a Savior. That salvation comes only through a faith relationship with Jesus Christ, the Savior, as a person repents of sin and receives Christ's forgiveness and eternal life. Salvation is instantaneous and accomplished solely by the power of the Holy Spirit through the Word of God. This salvation is wholly of God by grace on the basis of the shed blood of Jesus Christ and not on the basis of human works. All the redeemed are secure in Christ forever.

THE CHURCH IS GOD'S PLAN
The Holy Spirit immediately places all people who put their faith in Jesus Christ into one united spiritual body, the Church, of which Christ is the head. The primary expression of the Church on earth is in autonomous local congregations of baptized believers. The purpose of the Church is to glorify God by taking the gospel to the entire world and by building its members up in Christ-likeness through the instruction of God's Word, fellowship, service, worship, and prayer.

THE FUTURE IS IN GOD'S HANDS
God is actively involved in our lives and our future. *Through* His prophets, God announced His plans for the future redemption of His people through the life, death, and resurrection of His Son. *With* the call of the disciples, God prepared the way for the future of His Church. *In* Scripture, God promised that Jesus Christ will return personally and visibly in glory to the earth to resurrect and judge the saved and unsaved. As the all-knowing and all-powerful Creator and Judge, God can and should be trusted today, and with our future.

*[WEEK ONE]

DEVELOPING character

Biblical Passage: Matthew 5:1-10

Supporting Passages: Psalm 37:11, 41:1; Luke 6:20-23; 1 Peter 3:14

Memory Verse: Matthew 5:6

Biblical Truth: In the Sermon on the Mount, Jesus clearly defined new standards for the character and conduct of His disciples.

CONSIDER...

Defining moments. You've probably already experienced a few of them in your life. Some of them seem suddenly obvious, even though they've happened over time—such as finally becoming "an adult" living totally on your own. Others occur quickly—such as getting married, having a child, losing your job, or hearing the doctor's diagnosis. Defining moments mark a point in which things change and will never be as they were again.

At the height of Jesus' ministry, many people followed Him from town to town, listening to Him teach and watching Him perform miracles. As Jesus sat down to teach His disciples about His expectations for them, the crowds gathered before Him to hear His words. For those present, the day He delivered His Sermon on the Mount became a defining moment. While some listeners eagerly committed to His expectations, others decided the price was too high. These chose to walk away. As you study these verses, seek the answer to these questions: What does Jesus require from His followers? How do those characteristics differentiate Christ followers from those who do not know Him? How might other people respond to those who reflect Christ in their lives each day?

BLESSED A deep contentment based on God's favor. It is NOT a sense of happiness drawn from good luck or pleasant conditions. As a result, the person who is blessed experiences the fullness of God's presence in their lives, which leads to contentment in all circumstances.

how to be human

A *Teachable* MOMENT
Matthew 5:1-2

According to the custom of His day, Jesus sat down to teach His disciples. Although Jesus explained His expectations of those who wanted to become His disciples, His message was different from any other message the Jewish people had heard. Other teachers claimed that God's blessings were evident through a person's level of happiness and wealth. Jesus, however, proclaimed that true contentment was based on having a right relationship with God. Jesus began His teaching by describing the character of those who would become His followers. He emphasized that God's blessings were given to those who demonstrate meekness and mercy, who are poor in spirit, who mourn, and who are persecuted.

LISTENING TO JESUS

Read Luke 10:38-42. When Jesus arrived at the home of Lazarus, Martha, and Mary, Martha rushed to prepare a meal for the guests. Mary, however, took the opportunity to sit at Jesus' feet. He received her complete attention. As you journal below, consider: What priority do you place on sitting at Jesus' feet, and reading His words recorded in the Bible, and giving Him your complete attention? How do you respond when His words call for a change in attitude or action in your life?

PAUSE TO PRAY

Ask God to create an unquenchable desire within you for His Word and to provide time in your day to spend with Him.

week one: developing character

Followers of Christ recognize the depth of their spiritual needs. Matthew 5:3-5.

MIXED "Blessings" Matthew 5:3-5

Jesus' first words, "Blessed are the poor in spirit," must have shocked the predominately Jewish audience who had gathered. Devout Jews took great pride in the obedience to the smallest details of the Law, which they believed guaranteed God's blessings. But Jesus required His disciples to approach God with full awareness of their sinful condition and spiritual poverty that rendered them totally helpless before Him. As a result of their helplessness before God, Jesus promised, "Theirs is the kingdom of heaven." Only those who cry out for God's mercy on their sins would be granted forgiveness and entrance in His kingdom.

Jesus followed this astounding statement with another, "Blessed are those who mourn." The Greek word for mourn is also used to describe the grief felt when a friend dies. Jesus' followers express the same sense of devastation as they mourn over sin. They mourn over their own sins, over the sins of fellow believers, over the sins that permeate the world, and over unresponsiveness to the gospel. Jesus' promise, "They will be comforted," echoes the messianic message of Isaiah 61:1-3. Only God can relieve the grief over sin with the comfort of forgiveness.

In a world in which only the strongest rose to positions of power, Jesus said, "Blessed are the meek." Contrary to popular thought, meekness is not weakness. The Greek word for meek describes strength under control, and is seen in the balance between uncontrolled anger and complete passivity. Jesus revealed that His disciples accept God's sovereignty over the events in their lives without anger, dispute, or resistance. At the same time, they express righteous anger when others are wronged. Under the control of the Holy Spirit, the meek confront the sins of this world. Jesus promises, "They will inherit the earth," referring to entering the Promised Land (see Psalm 37:9-11). The meek do not seek control over earthly kingdoms but will be ushered into the kingdom of heaven.

PERSONAL inventory

WHAT DO YOU HAVE TO OFFER GOD?

HOW DO YOU GRIEVE OVER YOUR SINS?

HOW CAN GOD USE EVERYTHING IN YOUR LIFE FOR HIS GOOD?

GODLY SORROW

Read 2 Corinthians 7:8-11. In verse 8, Paul referred to an earlier letter written to confront sin among the Corinthian believers. Because of his convicting letter, the Corinthians expressed true sorrow for their sins. Worldly sorrow can be described as being sorry that one was caught, but not sorry for the wrongs committed. Conversely, godly sorrow expresses deep remorse for the wrongs committed and produces repentance along with the desire to see justice done. As you journal below, consider: Which type of sorrow do you most often feel? Which type of sorrow will produce the greatest spiritual growth in your life?

PAUSE TO PRAY

Allow yourself to see the sin in your life through God's eyes. Acknowledge your spiritual poverty before God and take time to mourn over your sin. Humbly ask God's forgiveness and allow Him to comfort you.

Wanting RIGHTEOUSNESS
Matthew 5:6

Followers of Christ seek Jesus to satisfy their righteousness. Matthew 5:6

In His first three statements, Jesus described the inward traits of His followers' character. People who realize their spiritual poverty, mourn over their sin, and exhibit meekness before God have reached the point of brokenness before God. According to Jesus, they now "hunger and thirst for righteousness."

Jesus used illustrations that His audience could easily understand. Jesus knew that within hours after eating, hunger and thirst would return. By using this illustration, Jesus emphasized that His followers would desire the Word of God with the same frequency and intensity as they desired food and water. Just as God provides water and food to satisfy physical thirst and hunger, He promises that those who hunger and thirst for righteousness "will be filled."

Because **People are God's Treasure**, God promises to satisfy our deepest desires for righteousness when we turn to Him. First, believers are judged righteous (or justified) when they receive God at the moment of salvation. Second, believers righteously live out their faith in a sinful world by leading righteous (or sanctified) lives as they rely upon God's righteousness while living out their faith in a sinful world. At the same time, believers long for God's righteousness to permeate our world, bringing His justice to all situations. Finally, believers are glorified when they enter heaven and the eternal presence of God.

Do you know how much water is in the organs of our bodies?

70% of the brain is water
83% of our blood is water
90% of our lungs is water
60% of our total body weight is water

[Source: http://ga.water.usgs.gov/edu/propertyyou.html.]

Our bodies signal us that we need water physically by making us:
– Less alert and less able to concentrate
– Slower to react
– Tired, headachy, and nauseous

What signals do we receive to let us know we need spiritual water?

THIRSTING FOR GOD

Read Psalm 42:1–2 and John 4:13–14. Just as the physical body must have water to live, the soul must be nourished by time with God. Jesus stressed that only He can satisfy our spiritual thirst. By drinking daily from the fountain of God's Word, our lives will overflow with His goodness and grace. As you journal below, consider: Do

how to be human

you recognize the signs of spiritual thirst in your life? When your thirst is quenched, do you offer drinks of living water to others?

PAUSE TO PRAY

Sit quietly before God for two minutes. Allow the rush of the day to fade into the background. Tell God how much you love Him. Ask Him to bless your devotional time today.

BEING righteous
Matthew 5:7-9

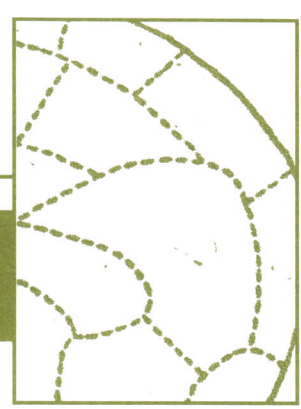

Followers of Christ reflect His righteousness in their lives. Matthew 5:7-9.

The diagram below illustrates the disciple's journey to brokenness before God. God meets each disciple at this point of brokenness and fills him or her with His righteousness. This inward change of heart results in an outward change of behavior. The attitudes and actions of believers reflect God's standards, which are higher than the world's expectations (see Isaiah 55:8-9). Notice the connection between the inward character traits and the outward actions.

INWARD CHARACTERISTICS	OUTWARD BEHAVIOR
poor in spirit	merciful
mourn	pure in heart
meek	peacemakers
hunger and thirst for righteousness	

week one: developing character

Jesus continued His discourse by observing, "Blessed are the merciful." The poor in spirit, humbled by their own sins, respond with mercy to others. Without the protective layer of pride, they recognize how easily someone can fall victim to sin, hurting themselves and others. They show mercy in many ways: meeting physical needs, extending forgiveness, and ministering with compassion to those who are suffering sin's consequences. As a result, Jesus said, "They will be shown mercy." Without the gift of God's mercy, no one can enter the kingdom of heaven.

When Jesus said, "Blessed are the pure in heart," He challenged His listeners to examine the motives of their hearts. Was their observance of the Law driven by religious obligation or genuine love for God? Were they fully committed to God's kingdom or torn between the desire to serve God and man? Disciples who mourn over their sins and the sins of humanity allow God to purify their hearts, making them completely devoted, morally and spiritually, to God. Since there is no hypocrisy within them, they reflect His righteousness in their thoughts, attitudes, and actions. Jesus promises these disciples "will see God." Through the eyes of faith, they see the glory of God as revealed in Scripture and by the Holy Spirit. Ultimately they will see the fullness of God's glory in heaven.

When Jesus delivered these words, Israel longed to be free of Roman occupation and oppression—even if their freedom was gained through rebellion and war. Yet Jesus said, "Blessed are the peacemakers," indicating that His disciples were called to make peace with others. As God's only Son, Jesus brought peace between man and God. He promised that disciples who extend that peace to others by sharing the gospel of peace "will be called sons of God." The meek possess inner peace because they have received God's forgiveness and have submitted to His will for their lives. Recognizing that sin destroys inner peace, they willingly share their source of peace with others and lead them to a reconciled relationship with God.

FULL OF HIS GRACE

Read Colossians 4:2-6. Paul urged his readers to devote themselves to prayer so they could recognize the open doors that God provides for sharing His gospel. Our recognizing the opportunity is not enough—we must boldly speak the truth. Paul stressed that our words must be backed by our actions. To draw on a familiar saying: we must walk the walk as we talk the talk. As you journal below, consider: What opportunities do you have to share the gospel? Are the words of your faith backed by the actions of your faith?

PAUSE TO PRAY

Thank God for allowing you to join with Him in carrying the gospel to others. Ask Him to strengthen your witness to others through both word and deed.

a DISTINGUISHABLE lifestyle

Matthew 5:10

Christ's disciples are called to a lifestyle that easily distinguishes them from people who do not follow Christ. By living according to the standards that Jesus established, they draw attention to His holiness and grace—and also draw attention to the sin that permeates the world. For this reason, Jesus said, "Blessed are those who are persecuted because of righteousness." While Jesus is honored by His disciples' lifestyles, the world often does not want to be reminded that God exists or that He has established standards for judgment. As a result, Christ followers will often suffer prejudice, ridicule, humiliation, discrimination, and even persecution. Christ reminds His disciples that "the kingdom of heaven" belongs to them.

REVIEW: Which beatitudes describe your relationship with God? Which beatitudes describe your relationships with other people? Do you find it easier to live in right relationship with God or with people? Which of these characteristics is God calling you to cultivate in your life? What will you do this week in response to His message?

SUFFERING FOR RIGHTEOUSNESS

Read I Peter 3:12-17. Peter suffered much for his devotion to Christ. His experiences show that God's eyes and ears are focused on His people, especially when they suffer for doing good. Peter encouraged his readers to remain focused on God and to respond with gentleness so that good behavior will cause attackers to be ashamed. As you journal below, consider: How do I respond when people attack me because of my faith? By responding with gentleness and respect, will I create an opportunity to share the gospel?

PAUSE TO PRAY

Pray that your thoughts and actions will reflect your faith in God. Pray for the strength to respond with grace to those who attack you. Thank God that He hears your prayers in the midst of suffering and ask Him to use that suffering for His kingdom.

*[WEEK TWO]

THE PERFECT RESPONSE to hatred

Biblical Passage: Matthew 5:38-48

Supporting Passages: Leviticus 9:18, 24:19-20; 1 Corinthians 6:7; Romans 12:9-21

Memory Verse: Matthew 5:44

Biblical Truth: Jesus demands that we respond with love to those who hurt us instead of seeking retribution and revenge.

CONSIDER...

Put me in, coach. Yes, boss, sign me up for that special project. Certainly, I'll be happy to chair that committee. Of course I can chaperone that student trip. How many times have you eagerly accepted a challenge only to discover that the demands were much greater than you ever dreamed! Perhaps the people in Jesus' audience who committed to becoming His disciples had a similar reaction when Jesus began to offer illustrations of what He required of them.

Throughout His sermon, Jesus continued to challenge the status quo and to raise the bar of expectations of how His followers should act. Nothing that He said was easy to do. Everything that He demanded required changes in both attitude and actions. As you study these verses, seek to answer these questions: Do these teachings make you uncomfortable? Why? If you had a one-on-one conversation with Jesus, what changes would He expect of you?

TEACHING HARD LESSONS

Immediately after describing the character of His disciples, Jesus warned them that they would suffer insults and persecution for their faith. He encouraged them to focus on their great reward in Heaven instead of allowing temporary earthly suffering to threaten their commitment to Him. But Jesus didn't call His disciples to persevere silently. He challenged them to "let your light shine before men, that they may see your good deeds and praise your Father in heaven" (Matthew 5:16). He then provided several illustrations that would allow His disciples to reflect His love to a world filled with anger, hurt, hatred, abuse, and persecution.

LET YOUR *Light* SHINE
read Matthew 5:13-16

Jesus commanded His followers to become salt and light in this world. By their actions, disciples reflect the love of Christ to a watching world. When believers fail in this task, they are losing their saltiness or hiding their lamp, which makes them useless in His hands. By living according to His commands, believers draw others to God. As you journal below, consider: Describe ways in which you have hidden your faith. Describe ways in which you have reflected Jesus to others. Renew your commitment to allowing your faith in Jesus to shine through your daily actions.

PAUSE TO PRAY

Thank God for believers who were used by Christ to draw you to Him. Ask Him to use you to light the way for others to find Him.

> *We are called to ignore insults instead of seeking retaliation or revenge. Matthew 5:38-40.*

RESPONDING *with Love*   Matthew 5:38-40

In the first illustration, Jesus referred to the *lex talionis*, or the Old Testament laws concerning vengeance, when He mentioned an "eye for eye, and tooth for tooth." Instead of supporting the victim's rights to seek retaliation, Jesus challenged His disciples not to resist an evil person. He continued this challenge when He urged, "If someone strikes you on the right cheek, turn to him the other also." In the ancient Near East, a backhanded slap on the cheek, accomplished when a right-handed person used the back of his hand to slap his victim's right cheek, was considered a greater insult than a slap using the open palm. Jesus called His followers to turn away from such insults instead of responding in kind.

In the next example, Jesus again referred to familiar Jewish laws. When suing for repayment of a debt, a person could demand the debtor's tunic or shirt, but he was not allowed to demand the outer cloak because it served as the debtor's covering or blanket at night (see Ex. 22:26–27 and Deut. 24:12–13). Surely Jesus shocked His disciples when He said, "If someone wants to sue you and take your tunic, let him have your cloak as well." Jesus urged His listeners to stop fighting for their rights and their honor, but to trust God to defend them and provide for their needs.

In both of these situations, the victim's immediate response is to get even with the offender. Jesus calls His followers to a higher standard. He challenges them to put aside their rights, to ignore the offense,

LEX TALIONIS This Old Testament directive was given not to require vengeance, but to limit retaliation. Based on instructions found in Exodus 21:23-25 and Leviticus 24:19-20, an injured person could seek vengeance against the offender, but his compensation could not exceed his loss. Although God's intention was to set limits for punishment, the lex talionis was often cited as the basis for demanding vengeance and compensation.

HOW DO YOU RESPOND TO INSULTS? check all that apply

- [ ] steam silently
- [ ] snippy comeback
- [ ] walk away in tears
- [ ] try to talk through the problem
- [ ] gently decline to engage the fight
- [ ] use humor to lessen the insult
- [ ] protest
- [ ] storm away angry
- [ ] call attention to their bad mood
- [ ] plot an appropriate retaliation

Which responses bring instant satisfaction? Which ones can diffuse the situation? How do you respond as Jesus requires when your emotions are demanding retaliation?

DO NOT repay

Read 1 Peter 3:8–12. Years after the Sermon on the Mount, the apostle Peter offered a similar challenge to members of the early Church. He reminded them of their high calling as Christ-followers. Instead of matching evil for evil or insult for insult, he urged believers to respond with love, sympathy, and compassion to people who attacked them. By seeking peace and harmony, they were sharing God's blessings with others. As you journal below, consider: What happens when you respond to evildoers according to your will instead of relying on the Holy Spirit? How can God use you to turn insults into compassion and hatred into love?

PAUSE TO PRAY

Thank God that He sees all things and recognizes when others attack you. Pray for the strength and self-control to respond with His love instead of retaliation. Ask God to use you to shower those who attack you with His loving compassion.

Wanting RIGHTEOUSNESS

We are called to give generously by exceeding the minimum requirements   Matthew 5:41-42.

Jesus was fully aware of the difficulty of His next challenge to His listeners. When He said, "If someone forces you to go one mile," He was referring to the demands of the Roman soldiers who occupied Israel. The very soldiers who imposed Roman rule on the Jewish nation had the right to demand that Jewish citizens carry their military gear for a distance of one mile. Jesus told His disciples, "Go with him two miles." Instead of displaying a grudging obedience toward their authorities, His disciples would respond by willingly carrying the despised burden for twice the required distance.

Jesus then transferred the command to give generously to other situations. He required His followers to "give to the one who asks you, and do not turn away from the one who wants to borrow from you." Jesus' command seems to recognize the borrower's request as valid and the giver's ability to meet the need. Disciples who give generously to those in need reflect the love and compassion of Christ, who gives generously to His people. This directive, however, is not without limits. When giving creates unmet needs within the family of the giver or when the recipient becomes complacent and dependent on his benefactor, then generosity has been misused. When exercised properly, giving generously to those in need allows them to overcome temporary difficulties, which enables them to help others in the future.

GIVING more than MONEY

Read Acts 3:1-8

As Peter and John entered the Temple for daily prayers, they were stopped by a lame beggar at the Beautiful Gate. The beggar asked for money, which Peter and John did not have. But they had something better to offer: healing through the power of Jesus. They interrupted their schedule, gave the beggar their undivided attention, and introduced him to Jesus. As you journal below, consider: Do people who ask for money always need money? When I can't give money, what can I give instead? How can I demonstrate the extravagant love of Christ through my response to others' needs?

PAUSE TO PRAY

Thank God for the many blessings He has given you. Take time to name 25 specific blessings in your life. Ask God to help you share generously with others from the blessings that He provides.

RESPONDING THROUGH *prayer*
Matthew 5:43-48

We are called to love and pray for our enemies and those who persecute us. Matthew 5:43-48.

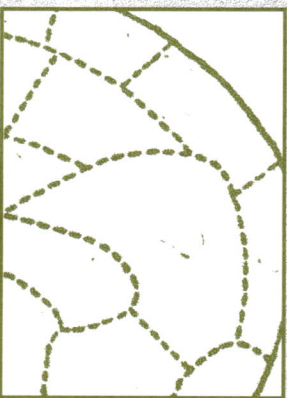

In His next statement, Jesus again raised an ordinary command to the level of extraordinary challenge. The Jews were familiar with the Law's requirement to love their neighbor, but they didn't focus on the requirement to dismiss revenge or grudges (see Lev. 19:18). At the same time, they used the command to love their neighbors as permission to hate their enemies (a command not found in Scripture). Jesus commanded His followers to "love your enemies and pray for those who persecute you." Jesus wasn't asking them to befriend (phileo) their enemies by becoming like them. Instead, Jesus wanted His disciples to love (agape) their enemies and through this unconditional love to

how to be human

lead them to Him. He specifically asked them to pray for their enemies, for prayer changes the hearts of both the one who prays and the one who receives prayer.

Jesus reminded His listeners that God "causes his sun to rise on the evil and the good, and sends rain on the righteous and the unrighteous." As an instrument of God's love, believers are called to pour out that love on all people, just as God pours nourishing rain onto all who live on the earth. Jesus proceeded to point out the obvious: Showing love to those who love us in return is typical and expected. Even "tax collectors . . . and pagans do that." Jesus said that God's love is most clearly demonstrated when disciples express love toward those whom they would rather hate.

Finally, Jesus provided the reason for the Christian's higher calling: "Be perfect, therefore, as your heavenly Father is perfect." In this context, being perfect does not mean living without error or flaw. Jesus was not calling His disciples to an unreachable standard. Here, perfection refers to completion or maturity. As believers grow in their relationship with God, they will become more and more like Him. As a result, they will be able to express agape love to their enemies because they are able to draw upon the resources of the Holy Spirit to fulfill that command.

LOVE TRUMPS HATE Read Romans 12:14, 12:17, and 12:19-21.

Paul was an enemy of Christians before he met Jesus in a vision while on the road to Damascus. At that time he personally understood the power of love to destroy hatred. He urged fellow believers to resist the urge to exact revenge by choosing to show love to their enemies. He reminded them that love will triumph over evil. As you journal below, consider: How do I respond to my enemies? Will those actions alleviate the animosity between us? How could the love of Christ change this situation?

PAUSE TO PRAY

Thank God that the power of His love is greater than any evil known to man. Ask Him to help you identify everyone whom you have treated as an enemy. Pray that He will bring healing to those relationships through the power of His love released in you and through you to the other people.

LOVE: the higher calling

By drawing attention to their flawed interpretation of various requirements of the Law, Jesus revealed that love was the guiding (and missing) principle behind those laws. Whereas the Jews interpreted the *lex talionis* as the basis for vengeance, Jesus emphasized that the laws were given to limit revenge. He then challenged His followers to forego retaliation entirely as an act of love toward those who offended them. When demands for obedience or financial assistance are made, Jesus urged His followers to respond by going the extra mile and by giving generously beyond the basic requirements. Finally, Jesus corrected their faulty belief that the command to love their neighbor included permission to hate their enemies. As Jesus set down the parameters for His disciples' higher calling, He called them to love others just as much as He loved them. Through His life and ministry, Jesus demonstrated that love was greater than law. He then challenged His disciples to live by the greater law of love.

REVIEW: Jesus places a high calling on His disciples. From this lesson, which of His expectations do you think will be the hardest for you to meet? Which ones will be easiest to meet? Is it possible to meet any of these expectations without the power of the Holy Spirit working in you? If you could lead every one of your enemies to faith in Christ, how would that change your world? What impact could that have on your community and country? Now that you know more of what Jesus requires of His disciples, are you ready for the challenge? Will you equip others to embrace that challenge with you?

LOVE GOD, LOVE NEIGHBOR

Read Matthew 22:36-40. When the Pharisees wanted to test Jesus' knowledge of the Law, they asked, "Which is the greatest commandment in the Law?" Jesus answered, "Love." He emphasized the necessity of loving God with all their heart, soul, and mind. He challenged them to love their neighbors as they loved themselves. As you journal below, consider: Is my relationship with God based on love or duty? Do I worship Him in love or obey Him because I fear Him? Does love flavor my relationships with others?

PAUSE TO PRAY

Thank God for His great love for you—love so great that He allowed His Son, Jesus, to die in your place. Ask God to show you ways to reflect His great love as you interact with all types of people in your family, church, workplace, and community.

week two: the perfect response to hatred

*[WEEK THREE]

SERVING WITH pure motives

Biblical Passage: Matthew 6:1-4

Supporting Passages: Romans 12:3-8

Memory Verse: Matthew 6:1

Biblical Truth: Jesus demands that we act out of pure motives.

CONSIDER...

How many times have you heard someone use the excuse, "Everyone in that church is a hypocrite," as a reason to refuse to attend church? How many times have you applied that same charge to a fellow believer who boldly "talks the talk" but repeatedly fails to "walk the walk"? Have you ever wondered why it is so easy for Christians to earn a reputation as hypocrites?

In the first century, the Pharisees and other religious leaders had earned the respect and admiration of many of the Jews. Through their public displays of giving, praying, and fasting, many were convinced of their obedience to God. Then Jesus arrived on the scene and began to call these religious leaders hypocrites! He said that they were simply going through the motions and performing spiritual tasks on their daily checklist while their hearts were far from God. As you study Jesus' words, discover the difference between a hypocrite and a devoted follower of Christ. Contemplate how different our churches would be if every believer served God with pure motives. Then ponder the difference that the Church could make in this world if that were the case.

Questionable MOTIVES

Jesus challenged His followers to reflect Christ in their lives by responding according to His character to stressful situations. He urged them to ignore insults, forego retaliation, give generously to those in need, and love and pray for their enemies. But Jesus also recognized the tendency for His followers to create a checklist of behaviors that would prove their devotion to Him. In fact, the Jewish people had long considered giving to the poor, prayer, and fasting as signs of devotion to God. While some Jews probably practiced these spiritual disciplines as a result of their commitment to God, many others tried to prove their righteousness through public displays of good works. Jesus reminded His listeners that people may be impressed by such visible acts of righteousness, but God is never fooled. He alone is able to discern the motives of the heart.

NO HIDDEN MOTIVES

Read 1 Chronicles 28:9 and Proverbs 16:2. As David gave his son Solomon the plans for building God's Temple in Jerusalem, he reminded Solomon that God searches every heart and understands every motive. He assured Solomon that those who seek God will find Him, while those who forsake God will be rejected by Him. Solomon later acknowledged the truth of David's words by recognizing that God weighs a person's motives. As you journal below, consider: Why do you help those in need? Is it comforting or scary to know that God understands your motives better than you do?

PAUSE TO PRAY

Ask God to reveal your true motivation for sharing the resources that He has given you with those in need. Pray that future gifts will be made to others because God has given you the desire to help.

week three: serving with pure motives

When we give to impress people, we will receive our reward from people. Matthew 6:1-4.

EMPTY *Rewards*

Matthew 6:1-4

Jesus cautioned His followers to avoid the temptation to perform "acts of righteousness" simply to impress those who might be watching. His words must have confused His audience, since He had just encouraged them to let their light shine before men. In His earlier directive, He indicated that God's love would be evident in their character and their lifestyle. Now He warned them not to become self-righteous by calling attention to their religious observances. He assured them that God provides no rewards for self-righteous posturing.

HYPOCRITE (HUPOKRITES) The Greek word translated as "hypocrite" actually means "actor." In Greek plays, the actors wore masks as they impersonated different characters. In time, the term was used for those who played different roles within their lives. Three types of hypocrites were recognized: 1) the hypocrite who intentionally deceives others while wearing the facade of goodness; 2) the hypocrite who convinces himself that his actions are true, but fails to fool others; and 3) the hypocrite who deceives himself and others into believing that his actions are pleasing to both God and man.

By saying, "When you give to the needy," Jesus acknowledged the importance of giving and His expectation that His followers care for those in need. But He forbade flashy giving with His next words: "Do not announce it with trumpets, as the hypocrites do in the synagogues and on the streets, to be honored by men." Whether Jesus was referring to actually blowing trumpets, the noisy rattle of coins tossed ceremoniously into a collection box, or the metaphorical equivalent of announcing one's generosity, He condemned giving as a way of drawing attention to oneself. Those who give to be honored by men "have received their reward in full."

Can churches encourage people to give simply for the sake of recognition? If so, how?

how to be human

CHEERFUL GIVING

Read 2 Corinthians 9:6-12. Giving should not be done reluctantly or under compulsion, to earn approval or recognition, or to entice God to provide more. God loves cheerful givers, those who give to others as an expression of their thankfulness to God for supplying abundantly for their needs. Because these givers trust God to supply their needs, they do not hesitate to share His supply with others. As you journal below, consider: What does your willingness to give reveal about your trust in God's provision? How do you determine when and how much to give away?

PAUSE TO PRAY

Thank God for providing for your daily needs. Pray that He will enable you to become good a steward of His resources as you determine how much to keep and how much to give away.

God's REWARDS

When we give to serve God, we will receive our reward from God Matthew 6:3-4.

As His followers fulfill their obligation to give to those in need, Jesus wanted them to keep in mind: "Do not let your left hand know what your right hand is doing." By using this familiar proverb, Jesus emphasized the importance of giving secretly, without demanding recognition or praise from others. Those who follow Christ should be so filled with His love and compassion for people that they obey His prompting to give thoughtlessly and effortlessly, scarcely aware of their actions.

As a result, Jesus explained, "Your Father, who sees what is done in secret, will reward you." Christ's followers cannot use this statement to manipulate God into providing desired rewards in return for human generosity. Rather, the disciple trusts God to determine the appropriate reward for his faithfulness. Like other promises, the reward may be received while living on earth or, ultimately, when face-to-face with God in heaven.

> What are some of the rewards that you have received from God as a result of sharing with others? What heavenly rewards might be awaiting you?

THE WIDOW'S MITE

Read Mark 12:41-44. Imagine that you are sitting beside Jesus, watching the people place their offering in the collection box. The wealthy throw in large sums of money that they will never miss. But the widow quietly gives two small coins to God. Jesus praised the widow's gift because she gave everything that she had, thereby demonstrating her complete trust in God to provide for her needs. As you journal below, consider: What does this story reveal to you about your offerings? Do you give to God only the funds that you will never miss or do you offer back to God everything that He has given to you?

PAUSE TO PRAY

Thank God for the example of the widow's trusting dependence on Him to supply her needs. Pray that He will use that example to teach you to trust Him more.

how to be human

QUESTIONABLE acts

Matthew 6:5-8, 6:16-18

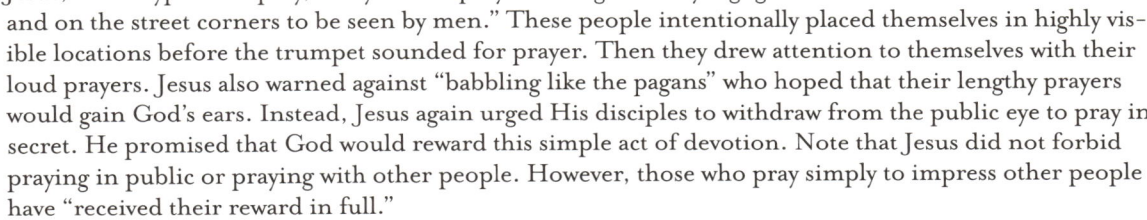

Jesus warned against other forms of spiritual boastfulness. Matthew 6:5-8, 6:16-18.

Jesus also compared the hypocrite's methods of prayer and fasting to ways in which His disciples should practice those spiritual disciplines. According to Jesus, when hypocrites pray, "they love to pray standing in the synagogues and on the street corners to be seen by men." These people intentionally placed themselves in highly visible locations before the trumpet sounded for prayer. Then they drew attention to themselves with their loud prayers. Jesus also warned against "babbling like the pagans" who hoped that their lengthy prayers would gain God's ears. Instead, Jesus again urged His disciples to withdraw from the public eye to pray in secret. He promised that God would reward this simple act of devotion. Note that Jesus did not forbid praying in public or praying with other people. However, those who pray simply to impress other people have "received their reward in full."

Fasting was commanded only on the Day of Atonement. Over the years, however, Jews had begun to fast for other reasons: to confess sins, to make special petitions, or to express anguish or desperation. During the time of Jesus' ministry, the Pharisees fasted two days each week. According to Jesus, these hypocrites would "look somber" and "disfigure their faces" to draw attention to their fasting. Since their goal was to earn man's recognition, "they have received their reward in full." Jesus knew that His followers would fast, so He urged them to groom themselves "so that it will not be obvious to men that you are fasting." The disciple fasts to express his devotion to God and doesn't need a human audience. He focuses in secret on his relationship with God, who "sees what is done in secret" and will reward him.

EXAMINE YOUR MOTIVES: Complete the statements below to reveal why you serve in various ways.

I give _____ because: _____

I attend _____ because: _____

I lead the _____ because: _____

I serve as _____ because: _____

I read my Bible because: _____

I spend time in prayer because: _____

What activities has God called you to do? What activities are you performing to fulfill your obligations or to meet others' expectations?

week three: serving with pure motives

FINDING TRUE RIGHTEOUSNESS Read Philippians 3:4b—9. Before becoming a Christian, Paul took great pride in his national heritage, his status as a Pharisee, his knowledge of the Law, and his legalistic observance of the Law's commands. When he met Christ, he realized that all these acts of righteousness were simply rubbish. Paul finally understood that righteousness comes only to those who place their faith in Christ. As you journal below, consider: Have I tried to substitute religious activities for true devotion to God? Which of these acts of service reflect God's presence in my life?

PAUSE TO PRAY

Thank God that He covers you with His righteousness because of your faith in Christ. Pray that your relationship with God will be so strong that you will become His instrument to serve others.

HEARTFELT acts

In the first century, hypocrites performed their religious acts of service loudly and publicly. They wanted everyone to recognize their obedience to God. But Jesus explained that God was not fooled by their efforts. God recognized them for what they really were: fancy shells that were hollow inside. For all their outward signs of spirituality, their hearts were far from God. Jesus urged His followers to focus their attention on pleasing God. From the heartfelt devotion that permeated their private life, they would exercise the spiritual disciplines of almsgiving, prayer, and fasting as acts of worship. In return, they would receive their reward from God.

CHEERFUL GIVING

Read 2 Peter 1:3-8. Peter tells us that everything we need for life and godliness is available to us through Jesus Christ. He encourages us to nurture our faith, adding goodness, knowledge, self-control, perseverance, godliness, brotherly kindness, and love. When these qualities permeate our character and actions, then we will be effective and productive citizens in His kingdom. As you journal below, consider: Do I spend enough time with God so that He can develop these qualities in me? When these qualities have been present in my relationships with others, have I been a more effective witness for Christ?

PAUSE TO PRAY

Thank God that He has called you into a relationship with Him. Ask Him to purify your heart and strengthen your faith in Him. Pray that you will become a faithful Christian whose desires of the heart match your actions.

Review

How would you define hypocrites and authentic Christians? For the most part, which group would you place yourself within? Which group do you believe is more prevalent in our churches today? What purpose does prayer and fasting serve in your life? Are these religious duties performed to earn respect and recognition from fellow believers? Or are they a natural action based on a heartfelt need to walk in daily relationship with Christ?

*[WEEK FOUR]

KINGDOM FOCUSED AND worry free

Biblical Passage: Matthew 6:19-34

Supporting Passages: Matthew 6:1–7:29, Luke 12:22-31

Memory Verse: Matthew 6:33

Biblical Truth: Jesus commands us to focus our attention on the Kingdom of God while trusting Him to supply all of our needs.

CONSIDER...

When you lie awake at night, staring at the ceiling, waiting for sleep to overcome you, what thoughts are racing through your head? Do you worry about our nation's economy? Do you worry about the value of your home or your investments? Do you worry about paying the bills this month? Maybe you've already experienced the worst—your home value, college funds, and retirement savings have plummeted, so you're worried about meeting future needs. What brings peace to your troubled thoughts? What calms your racing heart? What settles your mind and allows you to sleep peacefully through financial storms?

As Jesus continued to teach those gathered before Him, He addressed their worries about everyday needs and future possibilities. He challenged them to focus on the Kingdom of God instead of stressing out over earthly possessions. He revealed the futility of worry and urged His followers to trust God for their every need.

CHANGING THE FOCUS

Jesus clearly emphasized the character traits of those who accept the call to follow Him. By examining everyday concerns and emotions, Jesus challenged His followers to devote themselves wholeheartedly to His mission of establishing the Kingdom of Heaven on earth. He explained the significance of this call on a person's life by revealing ways that His followers should conduct themselves in this life. Even as Jesus taught His followers to give generously to others, He must have recognized the human tendency to give only when personal needs are met first. To redirect their thinking, He urged His disciples to focus their attention on things of eternal value instead of worrying about daily necessities and future possibilities. In return, Jesus promised, His Father would provide everything that they need in both this life and in the life to come.

FINDING THE RIGHT TREASURE

Read 1 Timothy 6:6–8. We run the risk of spending our whole lives accumulating stuff that we cannot take with us when we die. The stuff that we gather cannot guarantee health or happiness, and it certainly cannot defeat death. The greatest gift that we can find is contentment with our circumstances, whether we are wealthy or poor. By focusing on God, we find eternal treasure. As you journal below, consider: How much of your money and time is devoted to accumulating temporary stuff? Do you worry constantly about protecting your money and possessions? How can you redirect your focus to things of eternal significance?

PAUSE TO PRAY

Pray that you will understand the futility of gathering earthly riches. Ask God to capture your heart and focus your undivided attention on Him. Thank God for generously meeting your needs.

Matthew 6:19-24 WHERE IS MY *Treasure*?

We are called to store up heavenly treasures, not earthly possessions Matthew 6:19-24.

Jesus began by challenging His disciples to consider the treasures that they were storing up for themselves. Every material treasure that people try to accumulate can easily be destroyed by natural elements or stolen by thieves. Those who choose to store up such treasures for themselves must constantly be concerned with preserving and protecting them. In comparison, Jesus pointed out that those who store up treasures in Heaven never need to worry about protecting

week four: kingdom focused and worry free

their possessions. God will not allow anything to destroy those priceless eternal treasures. Jesus underscored His teaching by explaining that a person's heart will always be fully devoted to the things that he or she treasures, revealing whether he or she is devoted to the things of this world or to the things of God's Kingdom.

To emphasize His point, Jesus used another analogy, stating that "the eye is the lamp of the body." Whatever the eye fixes upon influences the life of the person. When the eye focuses on good things, the person will be focused on good things. Likewise, when the eye focuses on the wrong things, the person will be focused on the wrong things. In ancient Jewish writings, the eye was often treated as equivalent to the heart. Those who set their eye on God's Kingdom will devote their hearts to serving Him. Jesus then drew His explanation to its logical conclusion: "No one can serve two masters." People cannot serve God and money equally; one will always receive the greater devotion while the other will be ignored or despised. Jesus clearly taught that His followers must make the ultimate choice to focus on His Kingdom by choosing to forego the accumulation of material possessions.

> How can an obsession with wealth and material possessions prevent someone from serving God? How can devotion to God or to money be measured?

SHARING GOD'S PROVISIONS

Read 1 Timothy 6:17-19. As Christians, we are not forbidden to have material possessions, but we are urged to use them for God's purposes. Instead of putting our hope in worldly riches, we should put our hope in the God who provides those riches. Instead of becoming arrogant or hoarding our wealth, we are commanded to humbly share it with others. As you journal below, consider: Am I trusting God for everything or striving to make it on my own? Is God's generosity toward me being generously shared with others?

PAUSE TO PRAY

Thank God for providing for your daily needs. Ask God to help you hold your earthly wealth in an open palm, allowing Him to use the resources that He has given you for His purposes.

worry (merimnao) This Greek word means "to have a divided mind," "to be overly anxious," or "to have anxiety." It is the opposite of peace and wellbeing. Dictionary.com provides a vivid picture of the damaging effects of worry: "to seize, especially by the throat, with the teeth and shake or mangle, as one animal does another."

WHO WILL Take Care of Me?

We are called to trust God's provision, not worry about everyday needs. Matthew 6:25-30.

Jesus commanded His followers to stop worrying about food, drink, and clothing. His reasoning? The life God had given them was more valuable than the food needed to sustain it; the body was more important than the clothes covering it. To illustrate His point, He explained the great care that God gives to feeding "the birds of the air" and to clothing the lilies and "the grass of the field." Jesus reminded His followers that the birds "do not sow or reap or store away in barns" and that the lilies "do not labor and spin." They simply do what God created them to do. Jesus' followers, who are much more valuable than the birds, lilies, and grass, should concentrate on the Kingdom of God while trusting God to provide for their daily needs.

For those who still questioned the validity of His words, Jesus added, "Who of you by worrying can add a single hour to his life?" Jesus' ancestor, King David, also emphasized that God sustains life: "All the days ordained for me were written in your book before one of them came to be" (Ps. 139:16). Jesus urged His followers to forego the worry that could distract them from their mission. When believers are focused on building the Kingdom, they will witness God's actions in this world and quickly realize that worrying about basic necessities reveals a tremendous lack of faith in God.

DO YOU RECOGNIZE THE COMMON SYMPTOMS OF STRESS?

- rapid heartbeat
- headache
- upset stomach
- sweaty palms
- stiff neck and shoulders
- exhaustion
- difficulty concentrating
- worry
- anxiety attacks
- losing temper easily
- irritable
- weakened immune system
- high blood pressure
- heart disease
- heart attack
- acne

REPLACE WORRY WITH PEACE

Read Philippians 4:6–7. Worry consumes much of our mental energy, leaving us exhausted, stressed, and cranky. God offers a solution for worry. Whenever worries attack, we are urged to turn them over to Him in prayer. We have the privilege of asking God to handle every situation that makes us anxious. Convinced that He will sustain us, we experience His peace through every storm. As you journal below, consider: Do I allow my worries to consume me? Or do I turn everything over to God with full trust that He will sustain me?

PAUSE TO PRAY

Praise God for knowing your needs even before you express them. Surrender your worries to God in prayer. Ask Him for His peace so that you can face those worries with confidence.

Matthew 6:31-34 — WHAT SHALL I *seek*

We are called to focus on His kingdom, not agonize over this one. Matthew 6:31-34.

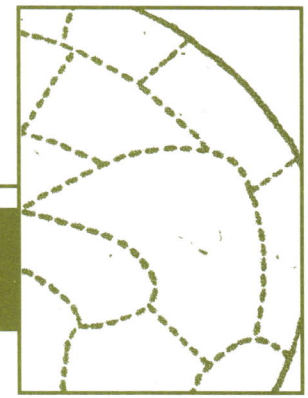

Jesus revealed a final compelling argument against worry. He cautioned believers to not act like the pagans who "run after all these things," but to trust their "heavenly Father" who "knows that you need them." Jesus' words contained a twofold message for His followers. First, the pagans (those who do not worship God) spend their time chasing after earthly treasure because they are not concerned with spiritual matters. Second, the idols and foreign gods that many pagans worshipped were often viewed as unpredictable and selfish. Pagan worshipers were constantly trying to appease these gods, yet they had little confidence that they would receive their gods' favor. In stark contrast to these pagan practices, followers of Christ can trust that their Heavenly Father, who already knows their needs, will generously provide for them.

Jesus called His followers to a distinctly different lifestyle from the pagans. Through their trust in God's provision, believers reveal that God is worthy of their worship and trust. By seeking "His kingdom and His righteousness," believers demonstrate their assurance that God will meet their needs. By committing themselves to a lifetime of service to God, believers testify to the surpassing joy of knowing God and striving to live according to His commands. Jesus concludes His instructions by reminding His followers of the importance of consistently walking with God. Believers should not "worry about tomorrow, for tomorrow will worry about itself." This is a reminder of the dangers of worrying about things that may never happen. Furthermore, believers must trust that God's grace is sufficient for the troubles of each day.

Seek GOD

Read Jeremiah 29:11–13. Even as God allowed the nation of Israel to endure extremely difficult times, He continued to assure His people of His loving purposes for their lives. Whatever we may face, we can trust that God's ultimate plan always gives us hope for the future. We can face anything as long as we seek Him with all of our hearts. He promises that we will always find Him. As you journal below, consider: Am I seeking God and His righteousness? Am I trusting Him to give me hope in all circumstances?

PAUSE TO PRAY

Thank God that He promises to respond to you whenever you seek Him with all of your heart. Spend time today basking in the warmth of His love. Pray that your heart will remain fixed on Him.

BEING different

Throughout all of time, people have been concerned with the basic needs of survival. For those who find some measure of success, worries about survival quickly become worries about accumulating material possessions to guarantee a life of comfort and pleasure. Jesus challenged His followers to focus on things of much greater value. Believers are called to live differently from those who are not part of God's family. Where unbelievers struggle to accumulate earthly treasures, Jesus calls His followers to accumulate treasures in Heaven. Where unbelievers worship the god of money, Jesus calls His followers to worship the God of the universe who holds all things under His control. Where unbelievers worry about basic needs, Jesus calls His followers to trust God for everything. Believers who focus their attention on the Kingdom of God by seeking Him and His righteousness reveal His glory to the world.

how to be human

REPLACE WORRY WITH PEACE

Read Psalm 145:13-20. God's kingdom is everlasting, His dominion is eternal, and He is faithful to every one of His promises. Because of His love for everything that He created, He provides everything needed for this life. God promises to be near to us when we seek Him. He promises to fulfill the desires of our heart. As you journal below, consider: Have you placed your trust in temporary riches or in the eternal God? Do you rely on His strength or your own?

PAUSE TO PRAY

Thank God for His faithfulness to His promises. Pray that you will surrender the desire to do everything on your own so that you can fully trust Him to provide for your needs.

Review

Jesus taught that worrying about life's necessities reveals that a believer has little faith in God. After reading this passage, how would you define worry? Has the habit of worry become deeply entrenched in your life? If so, what will you need to do to break the worry habit? How has God demonstrated that He is worthy of your complete trust? Does your walk with Him demonstrate that trust to others? What types of treasures are you accumulating? Are they subject to decay and theft or are they protected by God in heaven?

*[WEEK FIVE]

THE DANGERS OF judging others

Biblical Passage: Matthew 7:1-6

Supporting Passages: Luke 6:37-42

Memory Verse: Matthew 7:3

Biblical Truth: Jesus commands us to focus on removing the sins in our own lives instead of pointing out the sins of others.

CONSIDER...

What happens to the Body of Christ when individual believers begin to pass judgment on other members of the Church? Perhaps you've watched in disbelief as someone whose walk with Christ you admired became trapped in sinful behavior that brought hurt and devastation to their family. Did you respond by criticizing their failures or by reaching out with grace in hopes of restoring their relationship with Christ and fellow Christians? Perhaps you've despaired as your children made choices for their lives that did not include following Christ and His commands. Did you give up on them, or did you continue to speak the truth in love with the hope that they would return to the faith? Maybe you have faltered in your walk with Christ and felt the crushing weight of judgment and condemnation from fellow believers. Did you find the pathway back to Christ blocked by judgmental Christians or lined with compassionate people who knew that God could forgive and restore you to Him?

Jesus recognized the human capacity for judging others. Based on the self-righteous actions of the Jewish religious leaders, Jesus could easily foresee times when one or another of His disciples might compare his walk with Christ with another believer's apparent failures. Jesus warned His followers of the dangers of passing judgment on fellow believers.

hypocritical JUDGEMENT

Jesus began His address to the crowd by describing the character of someone committed to following Him (Matt. 5). He then described the personal relationship with Him that marks the Christian life (Matt. 6). In this final section of the Sermon on the Mount, Jesus began to describe how His followers should interact with other believers as well as those who do not know Him. Jesus had called the Jewish religious leaders "hypocrites" because they were performing their acts of righteousness to impress a human audience. Now He turned His attention to His followers. To avoid being painted with the same label, Christ's disciples were told that they must focus their attention on their obedience to Christ instead of judging the faithfulness of fellow believers.

DON'T JUDGE YOUR BROTHER

Read Romans 14:10-13. Paul reminded fellow believers that only God is qualified to judge the hearts and actions of people. Instead of believers judging fellow believers or putting stumbling blocks between them and God, Paul exhorted every believer to remember that they will give an account of their actions to God. As you journal below, consider: Am I guilty of judging others' commitment to Christ in my mind, in front of other people, or by confronting them? Have I placed a stumbling block between them and God? Am I ready to account for these actions to God?

PAUSE TO PRAY

Ask God to reveal any critical and judgmental attitudes that you have developed toward other Christians. Ask God to forgive these attitudes and to replace them with compassion for others.

We cannot judge others because God will judge us by the same standards. Matthew 7:1-2.

THE JUDGES ARE *Judged*

Matthew 7:1-2

Jesus began by bluntly telling His followers, "Do not judge, or you too will be judged." Some have interpreted this phrase to mean that believers should never judge any person, any teaching, or any action. Yet that interpretation does not seem to fit within the boundaries of other statements that Jesus made about judging. Consider these examples: In Matthew 7:15–16, Jesus advised His followers to beware of false prophets, who can be identified by their fruit. In Matthew 18:15–17, Jesus told His disciples how to confront a brother who sins against them. Obviously, believers are expected to make some moral decisions, or judgments, using standards set by Jesus. So what types of judgment does this command forbid?

Disciples fully committed to Christ will develop the character traits and total focus on the Kingdom of God that are described in the preceding sections of the Sermon on the Mount. As a result, they might be tempted to judge (and subsequently find fault in and even condemn) fellow believers whose obedience to Christ seems less devoted than their own. Jesus explicitly forbade His followers to develop a self-righteous attitude that leads them to pass judgment on others' walk with Him. For those believers who dare to judge, Jesus explained that God will judge them by the standards they apply to others. By judging others, the believer demonstrates his understanding and acceptance of God's standards, which means that he cannot claim ignorance for failing to observe those same standards.

What happens to a church when some believers begin to criticize and condemn others? What message do those outside the church receive when they observe believers judging each other?

INVALID COMPARISONS

Read Luke 18:10–14. Observe the prayers offered by two men from very different stations in life. The self-righteous Pharisee considered himself better than sinners. The tax collector was afraid to draw near to the Temple or even to look up to Heaven. Recognizing the humility of one man and the pride of the other, Jesus indicated that the tax collector went home justified before God. As you journal below, consider: Do I approach God humbly aware of my sinful condition? What does my attitude toward God reveal to observers?

PAUSE TO PRAY

Confess any areas of pride in your spiritual life. Ask God to reveal ways that you have judged others by standards that you cannot uphold. Pray for God's forgiveness of these sins and ask Him to create a heart of compassion in you.

We cannot point out others' sins while ignoring our own sins. Matthew 7:3–5.

where is your **FOCUS?**

Even believers have the amazing ability to see clearly the faults of others while failing or refusing to see their own faults. At other times, believers intentionally demand a higher level of obedience from others than they require of themselves. To force believers to recognize these tendencies, Jesus used an exaggerated comparison to make His point. By warning His followers not to worry about "the speck of sawdust in your brother's eye" while ignoring the "plank in your own eye," Jesus demanded that His followers focus their attention on their own faults. Only when believers have faced the difficult task of removing sinful attitudes and actions from their own lives are they capable of helping fellow believers deal with the sins in their lives.

Jesus' commands were never meant to be a standard by which self-righteous believers judged others. Instead, Jesus (through the apostle Paul) urged believers to "examine yourselves to see whether you are in the faith" (2 Cor. 13:5). The prophet Jeremiah urged God's people "to examine our ways and test them" before confessing to God, "We have sinned and rebelled" (Lam. 3:40–42). In his discussion of these verses in his book, *Studies in the Sermon on the Mount*, Oswald Chambers suggested that believers who recognize God's grace in forgiving their "plank" of sin should be able to show compassion to those whose sins are mere "specks" in comparison.

week five: the dangers of judging others

List a few plank-sized sins that should be addressed in your life and a few speck-sized sins that are plaguing other believers around you.

How will defeating the "planks" of sin in your life equip you to help others confront and defeat sinful behaviors in their lives?

PLANK (dokós) The Greek word dokós indicates a large beam or rafter that can be as large as 40 feet long and five feet around and is used in a building.

SPECK (kárphos) The Greek word kárphos describes something dry and light, like a splinter, straw, chaff, or even a mote.

ALL SIN IS AGAINST GOD

Read Psalm 51:3-6. When Nathan confronted King David for his sinful behavior, David confessed his dreadful sins to God. He realized that his sins hurt people, but he also knew that ultimately his sins were an offense against God. Though David realized that he should be punished for his sins, he begged for God's forgiveness and cleansing. As you journal below, consider: Have you considered that every sin you commit is offensive to God? Have you humbly approached Him for forgiveness and cleansing? Have you made amends with the people who suffered as a result of your sinful behavior?

PAUSE TO PRAY

Confess your sins to God and acknowledge how those sins offend Him. Pray for His forgiveness. Accept the cleansing from sin that He offers. Ask Him to create a pure heart in you.

WISE witnessing

Matthew 7:6

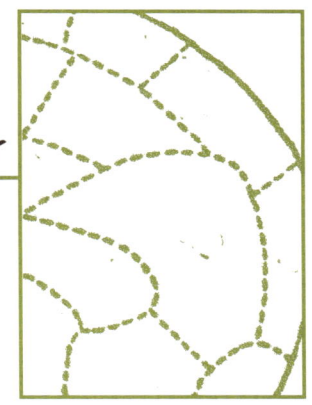

> We cannot force others to accept the gospel and obey Jesus' commands
> Matthew 7:6.

In His last directive in this passage, Jesus again shocked His disciples by saying, "Do not give dogs what is sacred; do not throw your pearls to pigs." According to ancient Jewish law, pigs were unclean animals. Dogs were wild animals, not beloved family pets. In Jewish speech, both pigs and dogs were derogatory expressions used to describe Gentiles or the ungodly in general. The "pearls" are the words of wisdom drawn from the gospel message. A cursory reading of this directive might leave Jesus' followers thinking that they should not share the gospel with those outside the Jewish faith. The New Testament, however, includes several accounts of Jesus sharing the gospel with Gentiles. In addition, Paul was later given the specific task of taking the gospel to the Gentiles. Therefore, another explanation must be determined.

Jesus called His disciples to exercise discernment when sharing the gospel with unbelievers or specific pearls of wisdom for a situation that a believer faced. In either case, the believer who shares cannot force another to accept God's Word. Those who have hardened their hearts against the gospel will reject the message and may viciously attack the believer. Believers must learn that there are times when they cannot reach someone. In those difficult and heartbreaking situations, believers should withdraw their witness and turn the matter over to God in prayer.

> Describe your efforts to witness to someone whose heart is hardened to the gospel. Why would Jesus tell us to refrain from witnessing to this person? How can Jesus use our prayers and our silence to change this person's heart?

THE ONLY qualified judge

Jesus didn't want His disciples to become self-righteous men and women who take upon themselves the task of judging others. Throughout His ministry, He repeatedly rebuked the Jewish religious leaders for that same offense. Jesus desires that His followers focus their efforts on developing a lifestyle focused on serving Him and His Kingdom. He calls His followers to a higher standard of holiness, not for the sake of checking religious duties off their list, but for the blessings of living in constant communion with Him. He challenges His followers to examine their own lives and to work diligently to remove the sins that hamper their relationship with Him. He urges believers to refrain from critical and judgmental attitudes that create division in the Body of Christ and cause unbelievers to refuse to accept the gospel. He reminds His followers that only God is qualified to judge a person's heart.

Review

Jesus warned His followers to avoid becoming critical and judgmental of others, for they would then invite God's judgment upon themselves. After reading this passage, when should a Christian exercise judgment and when should a Christian refuse to exercise judgment? When a Christian develops a self-righteous and judgmental attitude, what happens to the Body of Christ? How is attempting to force someone to accept or conform to God's Word another form of judgment? What is the proper way for a Christian to confront a fellow Christian who is caught in the trap of sin? What is the goal of this confrontation?

GOD WILL JUDGE

Read Psalm 96:10-13. In this passage, the psalmist is leading all creation (the heavens, the earth, the field, the trees, and everything in them) to praise the Lord. God rules over everything that He has created, and He will one day judge the world and every person in it according to His righteousness and His truth. As you journal below, consider: Would I rather trust God or another person to judge my life? Am I prepared to stand before God on the Day of Judgment? Have I trusted Jesus as my Savior so that God will not find me lacking?

PAUSE TO PRAY

Praise God as the Creator of the universe and as your Creator. Thank Him for your salvation found in Jesus Christ. Pray that you will resist the urge to judge others, reserving that task for Him alone.

week five: the dangers of jusging others

*[WEEK SIX]

BUILDING FAITH foundations

Biblical Passage: Matthew 7:24-27

Supporting Passages: James 1:22-25

Memory Verse: 1 Corinthians 3:11

Biblical Truth: Christ is the true foundation upon which we should build our lives.

CONSIDER...

Everyone faces difficult times in life. People often refer to these as crises or storms because they crash into their lives with such force that normal routines are destroyed, sometimes leaving their hopes and dreams for the future forever changed. Where do you turn when the winds of trouble roar through your life? Do you have a best friend who can keep the winds at bay and calm your fears? Or do you pull everything inside and try to march headlong into the storm, convinced that you are strong enough to overcome it on your own? Do you find it easier to surrender all hope and simply let the winds push you down and keep you there?

Jesus' followers are not exempt from the storms of life. They may endure the betrayal of a friend, persecution for their faith, financial hardship, death of a loved one, chronic or terminal illnesses, or many other types of storms. Jesus explained how His disciples can stand firm in their faith even when the storms inevitably try to destroy them. He emphasized that true disciples are those who walk in obedience to His commands every day. With their faith strengthened during the good days, they stand firm during the stormy bad days.

beware of false PROPHETS

Jesus warned His disciples to avoid the self-righteous tendency to judge others by standards that they were unwilling or unable to keep themselves. Jesus then described the proper way for His followers to exercise discernment when identifying false prophets. According to Jesus, believers can recognize false prophets by their fruit: Look at the actions of their lives that reveal their hearts. Just as a good tree bears good fruit, so a true prophet lives by and correctly teaches the Word of God. In contrast, the false prophet will be revealed when his or her actions fail to conform to Jesus' commands and his or her teachings do not match Jesus' teachings. Eventually the false prophet will be revealed as a foolish builder who did not base the actions of his or her life on everything that Jesus taught.

FAITH REVEALED BY FRUIT

Read Matthew 7:15-20. In this passage, Jesus explained the difference between a good tree and a bad tree as a metaphor for discerning true disciples from false prophets. The bad tree bears bad fruit and is incapable of bearing good fruit. The good tree produces good fruit; it simply cannot produce bad fruit. Likewise, the true disciple lives by the Word of God and teaches it with integrity. As you journal below, consider: What type of fruit is revealed through your actions and speech? If Jesus examined your life, what fruit would He keep and what fruit would be destroyed?

PAUSE TO PRAY

Thank God that He has given you the ability through His Word to discern true disciples from false prophets. Pray that your life will bear fruit that reveals Christ to the world.

BEWARE OF *False Faith*

Matthew 7:21-23

Jesus' words in Matthew 7:21–23 provide the background to understanding His next words. Jesus warned His disciples not to confuse true discipleship with the façade of faith that does not permeate a follower's lifestyle. His statement, "Not everyone who says to me, 'Lord, Lord,' will enter the kingdom of heaven, but only he who does the will of my Father who is in heaven" (Mt. 7:21), captured His listeners' attention. Many people will claim to be Jesus' disciples, but their lack of obedience to His will testifies to their false claim of faith. True disciples are overwhelmed by the grace of God that grants them eternal life. Because they love Jesus in return, they seek His will in all things. Their obedience is not born of compulsion or fear; rather, their obedience reflects the attitude of a grateful servant toward a worthy Master.

For those false followers who claimed to prophesy, drive out demons, and perform miracles in His name, Jesus said that He will one day respond by saying, "I never knew you" (Mt. 7:23). Jesus knows that some people can perform the work of true disciples even while their hearts are far from Him. With knowledge of Christ and His teachings and His power, they proclaim the Kingdom of God to others without first ensuring their place in the Kingdom by confessing Jesus as their personal Savior and Lord. Jesus' strong words should encourage His followers to examine their relationship with Him. Those who perform works usually identified with faith without first professing faith in Christ will not enter the Kingdom of God. The Kingdom is reserved for those who realize their need for salvation, trust Jesus as their Savior, and serve Him as Lord of their lives.

Is it possible to do the right things in Jesus' name and yet not have a personal relationship with Him? What are some ways in which people today convince themselves that they are Christians? How can someone evaluate whether they have confused religious activities with an authentic relationship with Christ?

how to be human

WALK AS JESUS DID

Read 1 John 2:1-6. John was reminded readers that sin was not the habitual pattern for those who claim faith in Jesus. Believers recognize that Jesus paid the ultimate price for their sins, and then they commit to following His commands. In these verses, John emphasized that love and obedience go hand-in-hand for those who follow Christ. As you journal below, consider: Is it possible to obey Jesus without love? Is love genuine if it doesn't result in obedience? What does your obedience to Christ reveal about your love for Him?

PAUSE TO PRAY

Spend a few minutes reflecting on God's enormous love for you. Pray that your love for God will be reflected in your obedience to Christ's commands.

True Faith STANDS FIRM — Matthew 7:24-25

Wise disciples build their faith on the Word of God; they can withstand any storm Matthew 7:24-25.

After warning His disciples that false followers will worship and serve Him without actually knowing Him and following His commands, Jesus offered encouragement to His true disciples. He used a metaphor to assure His disciples that building their life on Him would provide protection from the storms of life. Jesus emphasized the importance of not just hearing His words but also intentionally putting them into practice. Disciples will strive to obey all of Jesus' teachings, not just the easy ones or the ones on which they agree. When necessary, they will submit their will to His will so that His character can be infused into their lives.

According to Jesus' metaphor, the wise man built his house on a rock, or firm foundation, which withstood the storms. Likewise, the wise disciple will build his faith on the rock. Though he faces many storms in this life, the wise disciple's faith will hold firm. The word rock is translated from the Greek word *pétra*, and it describes a massive immovable rock that forms a strong and sturdy foundation. The same word was used later in Matthew's Gospel when Peter confessed Christ as the Son of the Living God (Matt. 16:16–18). Therefore, the rock or foundation of the disciple's faith is his or her conviction that Jesus is the Son of God. After establishing their faith on this firm foundation, disciples build their lives on the Word of God. Whenever a crisis strikes, though His disciples are battered by the storm, their faith remains strong and undefeated.

wise (phrónimos) This term means to think, to be prudent and sensible, and to develop wisdom in relationships with others.

foolish (moros) In the Greek, this term describes a foolish person as one who is morally worthless because of the flaws in his heart and character.

Many people say that they don't always recognize that God has prepared them to face storms until they have survived them. What things prepared you for getting through storms in the past? How did God reveal Himself to you during the storm? How did surviving the storm strengthen your faith in Christ?

FAITH LEADS TO OBEDIENCE

Read James 1:22–25. James emphasized that merely listening to God's Word is an exercise in futility. People who not obey the truths revealed in God's Word will quickly forget them. In contrast, true disciples examine their lives under the magnifying glass of truth and then intentionally put those truths into practice in their lives. As you journal below, consider: How do I respond when God's Word reveals changes that I need to make in my life? Do I live according to God's Word? Or do I sometimes pick and choose which commands I will obey?

PAUSE TO PRAY

Ask God to reveal where you have failed to obey His Word. Pray that He will give you the desire to obey every command, even those that you don't understand require much work on your part.

how to be human

THE FOOLISH *Fall Victim to the Floods*
Matthew 7:26-27

> Foolish people refuse to build their lives on the Word of God; they cannot stand against life's storms. Matthew 7:26-27.

Jesus completed His metaphor by explaining what happens to those who build their houses on sand. When the rains, floods, and winds beat against that house, it crashed because the foundation washed away from beneath it. Jesus explained that the foolish people who hear His words but refuse to put them into practice are not building their faith on a firm foundation. The foolish may agree that Jesus is God's Son, but they fail to accept Him as Savior and Lord. The foolish may agree that God's Word has value, but they fail to live by His teachings. When the storms of life swirl around them, foolish people quickly realize that their failure to walk with Christ daily leaves them vulnerable and unprotected—and their faith cannot withstand the storms.

Without a strong faith in Jesus, foolish people turn to other sources for help and comfort. They rely upon their own strength, their personal resources, or other people for help. In some cases, they survive many storms in life. Yet there is one final storm that they will not survive. No person escapes the storm of death; the foolish person will find that entrance into Heaven will be denied because of a lack of faith.

How might a foolish person and a wise person respond to these challenges?

Challenge	foolish	wise
unexpected job loss		
severe illness in the family		
ridicule for faith in Christ		
sexual temptation		
response to someone who hurt you		

week six: building faith foundations

DISCUSS: How do people without a strong faith in God cope with the storms of life? What happens when the things or people they rely upon cannot meet their needs? How can a wise disciple help others find the Rock who can help them face future storms with Him by their side?

FOOLISH BEHAVIOR

Read Proverbs 10:8, 10:10, 10:14, 10:18, and 10:23. These short pithy statements describe the actions of a fool and the resulting consequences. Foolish people refuse to accept commands or store up knowledge. Instead they cause grief with their lying lips and evil conduct. In the end, they will come to ruin. As you journal below, consider: Does part-time obedience provide a solid foundation for faith? Which foolish desires or behaviors in your life reveal a half-hearted devotion to God? Will this type of faith withstand life's storms?

PAUSE TO PRAY

Ask God to reveal areas in which you are currently walking in obedience to His commands as well as areas in which you are only partially obeying or even disobeying entirely. Pray that you will demonstrate your faith in God by seeking His counsel and obeying His instructions.

A RADICAL NEW WAY OF life

Throughout the Sermon on the Mount, Jesus called His followers to a radical new way of life. Those who choose to follow Jesus are challenged to develop a character and lifestyle that reflect His character and teachings. His disciples are urged to turn away from the patterns of behavior exhibited by those who do not know Him. They are called to dedicate their lives to Him and to building His Kingdom on earth.

Believers demonstrate their commitment to Christ by developing a deep and abiding relationship with Him that permeates their thoughts and actions daily. They are never satisfied with religious rituals and outward displays of piety. Their prayer life and service to Christ's Kingdom are based on their great love for Him. These disciples become fruitful witnesses of His love by refusing to develop self-righteous attitudes, choosing instead to realize that God's grace is sufficient to save anyone who calls on Him. By hearing and putting into practice everything that Jesus teaches them, His disciples understand how to be human—like God designed them to be.

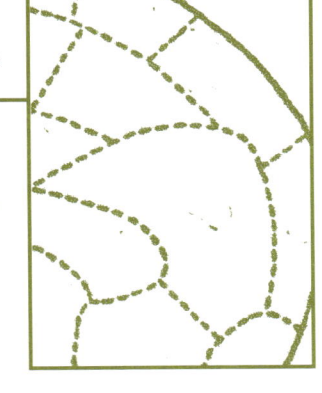

> Why did Jesus emphasized the necessity of practicing His Word? How has Jesus challenged you to further develop and practice your faith in Him? Are you convinced that Jesus can help you withstand any storms that this life throws your way? How would Christians impact their communities and the world if all believers lived their faith to the degree that Jesus calls them to do so?

FOOLISH BEHAVIOR

Read Psalm 119:9-16. The Psalmist stressed the importance of living according to God's words? He had hidden God's Word in his heart so that he could avoid the temptation to sin. By meditating on the truth and reciting God's commands to himself and sharing them with others, he continually strengthened his faith in God. As you journal below, consider: How much time do you spend reading, pondering, memorizing, and sharing God's Word? Are you storing up truths that God can use to sustain you during future storms?

PAUSE TO PRAY

Ask God to create within you an unquenchable desire to read and meditate upon His Word. Pray that He will reveal to you every day the promises that you need to withstand the storms you face.

life Bible Study

HELPING ADULTS KNOW CHRIST THROUGH HIS WORD.

FOR MORE INFORMATION, GO TO LIFE**BIBLE**STUDY.COM OR **CALL 877.265.1605**

OTHER STUDIES AVAILABLE FROM LIFE**BIBLE**STUDY®:

THROUGH THE BIBLE:
48-LESSON, YEAR-LONG STUDIES

YAHWEH: Divine Encounters in the Old Testament

CHRISTOS: God's Transforming Touch

EKKLESIA: The Unstoppable Movement of God

LIFE COURSES:
FOUR- AND SIX-WEEK STUDIES

- UNCOMMON: COMPELLED BY GOD'S CALL
- NO MATTER WHAT
- JESUS: IMAGE OF THE INVISIBLE
- FLAWED: IMPERFECT PEOPLE CHOSEN BY GOD
- HOW TO BE HUMAN
- COLLISIONS: MY EXPECTATIONS…GOD'S CHARACTER
- THE DARKEST HOURS: SEEKING GOD IN DESPERATION

lifebiblestudy.com
877.265.1605